THE ART OF COPYWRITING

HOW TO CREATE ENGAGING CONTENT THAT SELLS

SUBHASH CHAUDHARY

To all of the copywriters out there:

This book is dedicated to you. May it serve as a source of inspiration and guidance as you continue to hone your craft and find your voice. May it open your eyes to the possibilities of writing and the power of words. May it remind you that copywriting is an art form that requires creativity, skill, and dedication.

Thank you for all that you do.

Contents

Foreword

One of the most important skills in any profession is the ability to communicate effectively. Copywriting is no exception. From crafting compelling headlines to delivering engaging content, copywriters are responsible for engaging readers and inspiring action.

The Art of Copywriting provides an in-depth look at the many facets of copywriting. From the basics of grammar to the complexities of persuasive messaging, this book will help readers develop the skills they need to stand out in their industry.

Whether you are a novice copywriter or a seasoned professional, The Art of Copywriting offers valuable insight into the world of copywriting. With the help of real-life examples and step-by-step instructions, readers will gain the confidence and knowledge they need to become an effective copywriter.

So, if you're looking for a comprehensive guide to copywriting, look no further. The Art of Copywriting is your one-stop source for mastering the craft of copywriting and becoming a successful wordsmith.

Preface

As the title suggests, this book is all about the art of copywriting. It is meant to provide readers with a comprehensive guide to writing effective copy that will capture the intended audience's attention. With the help of this book, readers will learn the fundamentals of copywriting and how to write compelling copy that will engage and persuade their target audience. In addition, the book will provide readers with tips on how to craft engaging and effective copy for various purposes, from marketing and advertising to web content and more.

This book is the perfect resource for anyone looking to better understand copywriting and learn how to write effective copy that will produce the desired results. Whether you're a beginner or a seasoned copywriter, this book will help you hone your craft and become a better copywriter.

So, let's get started and dive into the art of copywriting.

Acknowledgements

I would like to express my sincere appreciation to the following people who helped to make this book, The Art of Copywriting, possible:

First, I want to thank my editor, Mr Uttam Kumar Thakur, my co-founder, for his patience and guidance throughout the entire writing process. His insights were invaluable, and I am deeply grateful for his unending support.

I would also like to thank my family and friends for their encouragement and enthusiasm throughout this project. Without their unwavering support, I would not have been able to complete this book.

Finally, I would like to thank the readers of this book. I thank you for your interest in the art of copywriting and I hope this book proves to be an interesting and beneficial read.

Prologue

Once upon a time, in a distant land, there lived a man who possessed a remarkable skill – the art of copywriting.

He could capture the essence of a product or service and craft it into words that resonated with readers, inspiring them to take action.

He was sought after by entrepreneurs and corporate giants alike, for his words had the power to change minds and drive sales. B

ut the man was a mystery, for he never revealed his name or whereabouts.

All anyone knew was that his copywriting was legendary.

This is the story of that man and his incredible journey to becoming the master of copywriting.

CHAPTER ONE

What is Copywriting?

Copywriting is the art of crafting words to create persuasive and engaging text. It is a form of communication used to influence, inform, or persuade potential customers or clients.

Copywriting is a powerful tool that can be used to sell products or services, build brand awareness, and generate new leads. At its core, copywriting is about creating compelling and persuasive messages that will be read and understood by the intended audience.

Copywriters are responsible for creating and developing the copy that is used to market a product or service. They are often the first point of contact between a business and potential customers, and as such, they must ensure that the message they craft is clear and effective.

When writing copy, the goal is to capture the attention of the reader and to create an emotional connection with them. Copywriters must be able to understand and communicate their client's message in an engaging way. The copy must be tailored to the target audience and aligned with the business's goals. Copywriting is an art form, and good copywriters are able to craft persuasive and engaging copy that resonates with readers and drives results.

The best copywriters can write engaging, informative, and persuasive copy. They can create copy that will capture the attention of the reader and compel them to take action. Copywriting is an essential part of any marketing strategy, as it is the most direct way to reach potential customers and convince them to take action.

The power of copywriting lies in its ability to create an emotional connection with readers and to influence their decisions. With the right copywriting strategies, businesses can increase their customer base, generate more sales, and build strong customer relationships.

CHAPTER TWO

Copywriting Techniques

Copywriting is an art form that requires creativity, clarity, and persuasion. It is the art of creating compelling content that encourages readers to take action. As a copywriter, you must be able to craft effective copy that is both informative and persuasive while maintaining a distinct brand voice. Several copywriting techniques can help you write compelling copy.

Here are some of the most important ones to consider:

1. Know Your Audience: Before you begin writing, it's important to know who you are writing for. Identify the age, gender, and interests of your readers, and tailor your copy accordingly.

2. Keep It Simple: It's important to keep your copy concise and straightforward. Don't use technical terms or jargon, and avoid long-winded sentences.

3. Focus on Benefits: People don't buy products or services; they buy the benefits that come with them. Make sure your copy outlines the features and benefits of the product or service you are promoting.

4. Use Power Words: Power words are words that evoke emotion or compel readers to take action. Examples of power words include: "amazing", "revolutionary", "guaranteed", and "free".

5. Use Testimonials: Testimonials are one of the most powerful copywriting techniques. They lend credibility to your product or service and help to convince readers that it's worth investing in.

6. Include a Call-to-Action: Every piece of copy should contain a clear call-to-action. This could be anything from "buy now" to "sign up for our newsletter".

These are just a few of the copywriting techniques you should consider when crafting persuasive copy. By using these techniques, you can create content that is both engaging and effective.

CHAPTER THREE

Writing Ads and Sales Copy

Copywriting is an essential part of advertising and marketing. Copywriting is used in the creation of advertising materials, such as brochures, websites, and postcards, as well as sales copy, which is used to promote a product or service. The goal of copywriting is to engage the reader and convince them to take action.

When writing ads and sales copy, it is important to keep the reader in mind. The language should be simple and easy to understand, and it should be tailored to the target audience. The copy should be concise and compelling, and it should include a clear call to action.

A good copywriter will also be aware of the customer's needs and how the product or service can meet those needs. They will be able to create a compelling story that will draw the customer in and make them want to learn more about the product or service.

When writing ads and sales copy, it is also important to use powerful words and phrases to evoke emotion and capture the reader's attention. The words should be chosen carefully to ensure that they are vivid and descriptive, and they should create a sense of urgency.

Finally, a good copywriter will also be aware of the latest trends in advertising and marketing, and they will be able to use the latest techniques to create effective copy. This includes using the latest technology and tools to create engaging visuals and interactive content.

By keeping the reader in mind, using powerful words, and staying up-to-date with the latest trends and techniques, a copywriter can create effective ads and sales copy that will capture the attention of the reader and encourage them to take action.

Writing for Web Pages

Writing for web pages is a special skill that requires an understanding of how people read and interact with web content. A successful web page should be well-organized, easy to read and scan, and persuasive.

When writing for web pages, consider the following points:

1. Keep the content concise and to the point. People don't have a lot of time to spend on a web page, so you need to get your message across quickly and efficiently. Keep your sentences short and avoid long paragraphs.

2. Break up text with headings, subheadings, and images. This will make it easier for readers to scan your page and quickly find information.

3. Use strong, action-oriented language. Your goal is to get the reader to take action, so use language that will motivate them to do so.

4. Use keywords. Strategically placing keywords throughout your content can help it rank higher in search engine results pages.

5. Link to other pages on your website. Internal links help search engines understand the structure of your website, and they also help readers find more information about a topic.

6. Make sure the page is responsive. Your page should look good on both desktop and mobile devices.

7. Optimize for search engines. This includes using keywords, meta descriptions, and other SEO best practices.

By following these tips, you can ensure that your web pages are well written and optimized for maximum impact. Keep in mind that writing for web pages is an art, and it takes practice to get it right.

CHAPTER FIVE

The Basics of SEO Copywriting

When it comes to copywriting, search engine optimization (SEO) is an important component. SEO copywriting ensures that your content is visible to search engine users. It involves the use of certain keywords and phrases that are relevant to your topic and are likely to be searched by users.

When writing SEO copy, it is important to keep the reader in mind. Your content should be interesting and engaging, while also hitting on the key points relevant to your topic.

You should also consider the structure and flow of your content. In order to get the most out of your SEO copywriting, you should research the keywords and phrases that are most commonly used by your target audience. You should also focus on writing quality content that is well-written, informative, and relevant.

When writing SEO copy, it is important to use headings and subheadings to break up your content and make it easier for the reader to skim and scan. You should also ensure that your content is optimized for both desktop and mobile devices.

Finally, you should use proper formatting to make your content more readable. This includes proper punctuation, spacing, and proper use of headings and subheadings.

By following these simple guidelines, you can ensure that your SEO copywriting is effective and drives the desired results.

CHAPTER SIX

Writing for Social Media

In today's digital age, social media is an invaluable tool for businesses and organizations to reach their target audiences. With over 3 billion active users across the globe, social media is a great way to engage potential customers and build relationships with them.

As a copywriter, you must know how to write effective and engaging content for social media. Your content should be creative, entertaining, informative, and persuasive. It should also be tailored to the specific platform on which you are posting.

Here are some tips for writing effective copy for social media:

1. Know Your Audience: Before you start writing, take the time to understand who your target audience is and what they are looking for. This will help you create better content that resonates with them.

2. Keep it Short and Sweet: People on social media tend to have short attention spans, so keep your posts short and to the point. Focus on a single message or idea and avoid long paragraphs of text.

3. Use Visuals: Visuals are key when it comes to social media. They help draw attention to your posts and make them more engaging. Use photos, videos, GIFs, and other visuals to communicate your message.

4. Use Hashtags: Hashtags are a great way to increase the reach of your content. They help categorize your post and make it easier for people to find.

5. Engage with Your Audience: Social media is a two-way street. Make sure to respond to comments and questions from your followers. This helps build relationships and encourages engagement.

Writing for social media can be a bit tricky, but with the right approach, you can create effective content that resonates with your audience. Keep these tips in mind and you'll be well on your way to copywriting success.

CHAPTER SEVEN

Writing for Different Audiences

The art of copywriting is more than just words on a page – it's an understanding of the audience you're writing for. Every audience is different and requires its own set of rules and guidelines. Knowing your audience well will help create content that resonates with them.

When writing for different audiences, it's important to be aware of the language they use and the topics they care about. There is no one-size-fits-all approach when it comes to copywriting. What works for one audience may not be effective for another.

For instance, if you're writing for a younger demographic, you might want to use slang or current pop culture references to engage them. On the other hand, if you're writing for an older demographic, you might want to focus on more traditional language and themes.

It is also important to consider how people from different backgrounds might interpret your words. Take into consideration any potential cultural or language differences that could affect how your audience understands your message.

Finally, keep your writing concise and to the point. Your audience's attention span is limited, so it's important to get to the point quickly and avoid unnecessary words or phrases.

By taking the time to understand your audience and write accordingly, you can create content that will have a lasting impact.

Writing for different audiences requires a thoughtful and tailored approach, but when done correctly, it can be a powerful tool for communicating your message.

Writing for Different Platforms

Copywriting is an art that is applicable to multiple platforms, each requiring its own unique style and approach. To be successful at copywriting, you must be able to adapt your writing to the platform you are writing for. In this chapter, we will discuss the various platforms and what to keep in mind when writing for them.

Print Media

Print media is still a popular form of advertising, as it allows you to reach a large audience. When writing for print media, it is important to keep your writing concise and to the point. Since print media is limited by space, you must ensure that your message is clear and succinct. Be sure to use simple language and avoid jargon, as it can be difficult to understand.

Web

The web is a powerful copywriting platform, allowing you to reach a larger audience. When writing for the web, you must be mindful of the medium and be sure to optimize your content for search engine optimization (SEO). Additionally, you must ensure that your content is engaging and easily readable on any device.

Social Media

Social media is an increasingly popular platform for copywriting, as it allows you to connect with a large audience. When writing for social media, you must ensure that your content is engaging, as it is often competing with other content for attention. Additionally, you must ensure that your content is concise and to the point, as users often skim through posts quickly.

Email

Email remains a popular platform for copywriting, as it allows you to reach a large audience with a personalized message. When writing for email, you must be mindful of the context and ensure that your message is engaging and relevant to the reader. Additionally, you must ensure that your message is concise and to the point, as readers often skim through emails quickly.

As you can see, many different platforms require different approaches when it comes to writing. As a copywriter, it is important to be able to adapt your writing to each platform and ensure that your message is engaging and relevant to the audience.

CHAPTER NINE

Copywriting Ethics

The success of copywriting depends heavily on ethical practices. The following are some of the ethical standards that every copywriter should adhere to:

1. Respect the privacy of the audience: It is important to respect the privacy of the audience and refrain from collecting information about them without their consent. It is also important to avoid collecting personal information such as addresses, phone numbers, or credit card numbers without their consent.

2. Respect copyright laws: Copying the work of others without their permission is illegal and unethical. It is important to respect copyright laws and avoid any actions that could result in copyright infringement.

3. Avoid deception: Copywriters should avoid deceptive techniques that are designed to mislead the audience. This includes false claims, exaggerations, and misleading information.

4. Respect the truth: Copywriters should strive to be truthful in their writing. It is important to avoid making false or exaggerated claims, or making promises that cannot be fulfilled.

5. Respect the rights of the client: Copywriters should respect the rights of their clients. This includes honoring the terms of contracts and not taking advantage of their clients.

6. Respect the rights of the audience: Copywriters should respect the rights of their audience. This includes not using language that is offensive or that could be viewed as offensive.

7. Respect the industry: Copywriters should strive to maintain the integrity of the industry by using best practices and avoiding unethical practices.

By following these ethical standards, copywriters can ensure that their work will be respected and admired. By maintaining a high standard of ethics, copywriters can ensure that the industry remains a source of trust and quality for both clients and audiences.

CHAPTER TEN

Copywriting Mistakes to Avoid

Copywriting is an art form that requires skill and knowledge, and it's easy to make mistakes. To ensure your copywriting is successful, it's important to be aware of the common mistakes to avoid.

1. Not Researching Your Audience: When writing copy, it's essential to understand who your audience is and what they want to hear. Spend time researching your target market and gathering insights into their needs and interests. This will help ensure your copy resonates with them and is more likely to convert.

2. Not Writing with a Purpose: Every piece of copy you write should have a purpose. Whether it's to inform, educate, persuade, or entertain your reader, make sure it's clear from the outset. This will help you stay focused and ensure your copy is effective.

3. Using Jargon or Buzzwords: Your copy should be easy to understand and engaging. Avoid using industry jargon and buzzwords, as they can be off-putting and confusing to your readers. Keep it simple and conversational and ensure your message is clear.

4. Not Testing: Before launching your copy, make sure to test it out on a variety of people. Ask for honest feedback and use it to fine-tune and optimize your copy. Testing will help ensure it resonates with your target audience and is more likely to convert.

5. Not Being Specific: Being specific and providing details will help your readers trust you and be more likely to take action. Instead of making broad statements, be specific and provide examples of how your product or service can help.

These are just some of the most common copywriting mistakes to avoid. As long as you research your target audience and write with a purpose, you'll be on the right track to creating successful copy.

Read More

Adler, J. (2016). The art of copywriting: A guide to crafting effective copy. New York, NY: McGraw-Hill.

Gillespie, P. (2012). The copywriter's handbook: A step-by-step guide to writing copy that sells.

Hoboken, NJ: John Wiley & Sons. KopywritingKourse. (2014).

The ultimate guide to copywriting. Retrieved from https://www.kopywritingkourse.com/copywriting-guide/ Strunk, W., & White, E. B. (2000).

The elements of style (4th ed.). Boston, MA: Allyn & Bacon.

Influencers To Follow

1. Ann Handley (@MarketingProfs) – Ann Handley is the Chief Content Officer at MarketingProfs and the co-founder of ClickZ. She is a bestselling author and an inspiring speaker. She is an expert on copywriting and content marketing and an influential voice in the marketing industry.

2. Neville Medhora (@NevMed) – Neville Medhora is the founder of KopywritingKourse.com, an online resource for copywriters. He is an experienced copywriter and has written copy for many Fortune 500 companies. He is a frequent contributor to Copyblogger and other industry websites and a prominent figure on Twitter.

3. Henneke Duistermaat (@HennekeD) – Henneke Duistermaat is an experienced copywriter and the founder of EnchantingMarketing.com. She is a popular speaker and an expert on copywriting and content marketing. She is also the author of several books and an active contributor to industry publications.

4. Joanna Wiebe (@copyhackers) – Joanna Wiebe is the founder of Copyhackers.com, an online resource for copywriters. She is an experienced copywriter and a sought-after speaker. She is an influential figure in the copywriting industry and an active contributor to industry publications.

5. Robert Rose (@Robert_Rose) – Robert Rose is the Chief Strategist at the Content Marketing Institute and a sought-after speaker on content marketing and copywriting. He is an experienced copywriter and a prominent figure in the industry. He is a frequent contributor to industry publications and an active voice on Twitter.

www.ingramcontent.com/pod-product-compliance
Lightning Source LLC
Chambersburg PA
CBHW070611170726
48004CB00017B/912